All about...

Dick King-Smith

Vic Parker

www.heinemann.co.uk/library
Visit our website to find out more information about **Heinemann Library** books.

To order:
 Phone 44 (0) 1865 888066
 Send a fax to 44 (0) 1865 314091
 Visit the Heinemann Bookshop at www.heinemann.co.uk/library to browse our catalogue and order online.

First published in Great Britain by Heinemann Library, Halley Court, Jordan Hill, Oxford OX2 8EJ, part of Harcourt Education. Heinemann is a registered trademark of Harcourt Education Ltd.

Editorial: Lucy Thunder and Helen Cannons
Design: David Poole and Geoff Ward
Picture Research: Rebecca Sodergren and Kay Altwegg
Production: Edward Moore

Originated by Repro Multi-Warna
Printed and bound in China by South China Printing Company
The paper used to print this book comes from sustainable resources.

ISBN 0 431 17988 3
08 07 06 05 04
10 9 8 7 6 5 4 3 2 1

British Library Cataloguing in Publication Data
Parker, Vic
King-Smith, Dick - (All About...)
823.9'14
A full catalogue record for this book is available from the British Library.

Acknowledgements
The Publishers would like to thank the following for permission to reproduce photographs:
Clarks Shoes p**18**; John Cleare p**10**; Michael Dyer Associates p**5**; Farmborough Primary School p**19**; Granada Media pp**22**, **29**; Ronald Grant Archive p**23**; Chris Honeywell p**4**; Hulton Archive pp**11**, **17**; Dick King-Smith pp**6**, **7**, **8**, **9**, **12**, **14**, **15**, **16**, **25**, **28**; Penguin Group p**20**; Mary Raynor / Victor Gollancz p**26**; David Samuel Robbins / Corbis p**27**; Mike Terry / Puffin Books p**21**.

Cover photograph of Dick King-Smith with his pet dog, Dodo, reproduced with permission of Penguin Books Ltd.

Sources
The author and Publishers gratefully acknowledge the publications which were used for research and as written sources for this book:

Amazon reader reviews –
www.amazon.co.uk pp**28–9**
Chewing the Cud by Dick King-Smith (Penguin, 2002) pp**11**, **20**, **21**, **24**, **25**, **27**
The *Guardian*, article by Julia Eccleshare (10 November 2001) p**8**
The *Guardian's* website – www.guardian.co.uk pp**22–3**
The *Independent's* website – www.independent.co.uk pp**22–3**
Random House Books website – www.kidsatrandomhouse.co.uk p**28**
Stories from the Web – www.storiesfromtheweb.org pp**28–9**
Tell Me About Dick King Smith by Chris Powling (Evans Brothers, 2003)

Fiction works by Dick King-Smith are cited in the text.

Contents

Who is Dick King-Smith?   4

Childhood in the countryside   6

Dick's war   12

A farm and a family   14

The stories start to flow   18

The successful author   24

Dick King-Smith on Dick King-Smith   26

Dick today   28

Timeline   30

Books by Dick King-Smith   30

Glossary   31

Index   32

Any words appearing in the text in bold, **like this**, are explained in the glossary.

The author and Publishers would like to thank Dick King-Smith for his invaluable help in the writing of this book.

Who is Dick King-Smith?

Dick King-Smith is one of the most popular authors writing for children today. He is best loved for his charming and funny stories about animals, such as *The Hodgeheg* and *Sophie's Snail*. Most famous of all is *The Sheep-Pig*, which was turned into the Hollywood hit movie *Babe*.

A late starter

Dick did not start writing until he was 54 years old! First, he was a farmer for 20 years and then he became a primary school teacher. It was Dick's farming days that gave him lots of ideas for stories. He wrote his first book, *The Fox Busters*, during his first summer holidays from teaching. Since then, Dick has won several top prizes for his books. He was even voted Children's Author of the Year at the British Book Awards in 1992. To date, Dick has had over 100 stories **published**, in many different languages, which have sold millions of copies worldwide.

Dick has had many books published over the years. Here are some of his best-selling stories.

Squawking or talking?

Some of the best children's books ever written have been about animals who can speak. For example, *The Jungle Book* (later used by Disney to make a movie) and the *Just So Stories* were written over 100 years ago by the famous author Rudyard Kipling. They are about animals living in the jungles of India who talk and understand each other. *Dick has followed in the* footsteps of Kipling and other great writers. He likes to call his brilliant tales 'farmyard fantasies'.

Pigs are among Dick's favourite animals. ▶

Factfile

★ Date of birth	27 March 1922
★ Star sign	Aries
★ Eye colour	Bottom of the duck pond
★ Hair colour	Grey-white or white-grey
★ Pets	At present: 8 chickens (named after a famous family of writers called the Brontës)
★ Hobbies	Washing up, walking, sitting in the garden, reading, and writing children's books
★ Favourite food	Bacon and eggs, fish pie with eggy sauce
★ Favourite book	*Barchester Towers* by Anthony Trollope
★ Bad habits	Snoring
★ Personal motto	'Count your blessings!'

Childhood in the countryside

Dick King-Smith's parents fell in love in 1920 and once married they settled in an English village called Bitton, between Bath and Bristol, near the Welsh border. Dick's father worked there in the family business, running a **paper mill**. Dick was their first child, born in 1922. Dick's brother, Tony, was born six years later.

▲ Dick loved to play outdoors when he was little.

The village of Bitton is deep in the Gloucestershire countryside. So Dick spent much of his childhood roaming about outdoors, exploring the fields and woods and lanes round about. He grew to love all sorts of creatures – from tiny creepy-crawlies to large farm animals. Dick also kept lots of pets, including mice, rats, guinea-pigs, tortoises, rabbits and budgies.

Pet name
'Dick' is not actually Dick King-Smith's real name. His parents named him Ronald Gordon King-Smith. (Ronald was his father's name. Gordon was the name of one of his father's friends.) When he was little, everyone called him Gordon (which he hated!). Then his parents began to call him the pet name 'dicky-bird'. Over the years, this shrank to 'Dicky' and finally became just 'Dick'.

Good grandparents

Dick saw a lot of his grandparents during his childhood. His father's parents lived just ten minutes' walk away. Granny King-Smith used to take Dick to church on Sundays. Afterwards, she made afternoon tea for the family and they played games together. Dick was a terrible cheat! 'Grampy' King-Smith had a huge butterfly collection and often took Dick on butterfly-hunting expeditions.

Dick's mother's parents, the Bouchers, lived a train ride away in a Welsh village called Dinas Powis in Glamorgan. Dick and Tony often went to stay with them during the summer. Their grandad was a fun-loving man who liked playing tricks on people. Granny Boucher often took Dick and Tony to the beach at Barry Island for seaside picnics. They liked exploring rock pools for sea creatures like crabs and starfish.

▲ Dick, aged four, with his great-grandfather, Granny Boucher, and his mother.

Schooldays

Dick was sent to a **boarding school**, Beaudesert Park, in the Cotswolds, when he was just nine. Like all the other new boys, Dick was terribly **homesick** to begin with. He had never been away from home before, and he missed his family and all his pets terribly. Besides, life at boarding school was very strict, with lots of rules to follow. The teachers were often tough and gave out hard punishments. However, once Dick had settled down, he enjoyed school.

▲ Dick, aged nine, in his school uniform.

When he was twelve, Dick moved to a boarding school in Wiltshire called Marlborough College. Dick has said that at school he was 'reasonably intelligent', but also 'reasonably lazy'!

What Dick says

Dick loved animals as a child. When he was not out spotting wild creatures, or looking after his pets at home, he liked reading about animals too. He also once said in an interview that he had:

'a toy farm which I played with endlessly ... I never minded much what went with what, so I included a giraffe among the dairy herd...'

Home for the holidays

During the school holidays, Dick and his brother spent most of their time with a friend called Jamie and his sister Margaret, who lived close by. They called themselves the Red Hand Gang. They liked to play cards and board games, and spent whole days exploring the countryside on their bikes.

A girl called Myrle

At his parents' party on Christmas Day in 1936, Dick met a girl called Myrle England. Myrle was fourteen, like Dick, and just as keen on animals as he was. She even bred budgies, just as he did. Dick was especially impressed because Myrle had a bull terrier dog she had taught to do all sorts of tricks. Dick liked Myrle best out of all the girls he knew – although he was annoyed that she could throw stones further than he could!

Myrle's family moved away a year or so later, but Dick and Myrle did not forget each other...

▲ Myrle England, aged eighteen.

▲ Dick enjoyed his time at Tytherington Farm, shown here.

Dick decides on a career

By the time Dick left Marlborough at eighteen, **World War II** had broken out. The British **government** began calling all young men to join the fighting. Waiting to be called was a terrible feeling. Everyone knew that if you went to fight, there was a big chance that you would be killed in battle. Dick had about a year to wait before he would have to go. His father suggested that he should start at university in the meantime. But Dick had had enough of studying books. What he really wanted to learn was farming.

In the early summer of 1940, Dick went to work at Tytherington Farm in the Wylye Valley, Wiltshire. In those days there were very few electrical farming machines. Dick had to **hoe** whole fields by hand and plough them by trudging a horse up and down. He had to heave huge bundles of corn on to wagons and lug heavy sacks of grain. Farming was very hard, tiring work, but Dick thoroughly enjoyed it.

A special visitor

That summer, Dick's old friend Myrle came to visit him at the farm. They had not seen each other for several years, but they got on just as brilliantly as before. As soon as the visit was over, Dick excitedly telephoned his mother. He told her that he had decided on the girl he was one day going to marry.

What Dick says

In his book *Chewing the Cud*, Dick explains why he wanted to be a farmer:

'I think I always wanted to farm ... the wish had two strong roots: to continue to live in the country and to work with animals...'

▲ When Dick started farming in the 1940s, most work had to be done by hand, like hay-making.

Dick's war

After a year at Tytherington Farm, Dick decided not to wait any longer for the **army** to call him. So many young men like him had already been sent abroad to danger and death that Dick felt guilty about still being at home. In the summer of 1941, during **World War II**, Dick went to an army camp at Caterham and asked to join up. He was **enlisted** in the Grenadier Guards and began training to be a soldier.

Dangerous times

Whenever Dick was allowed some time off from the army, he travelled to visit Myrle. She had joined the **Air Force**, to work spotting enemy planes. The couple were in love, but they knew that soon Dick would be sent abroad to fight. The worst could easily happen and Dick might never return home. Although Dick and Myrle were both just 20 years old, they decided not to wait any longer to get married.

Dick and Myrle on their wedding day.

A married man

Dick and Myrle's wedding took place on 6 February 1943. After just two days together, they had to return to their duties at their separate base camps. They were only allowed to see each other twice more before Dick was sent away to fight.

Fighting for his life

Dick arrived in the south of Italy in early September 1943. The countryside was crawling with enemy German soldiers. Dick was in charge of a **platoon** who had to march northwards, fighting all the way. Week after week, the soldiers battled their way up and down mountains as bombs exploded all around them, and waded through rivers, dodging bullets. It was extremely dangerous and many of Dick's friends were wounded or killed.

Dick lasted out for eleven months of non-stop fighting. Then he and his men were fired on in a wood on a hilltop. Dick was hit by an exploding **hand grenade**. It ripped into his legs, stomach and bottom, injuring him terribly. Eight other British soldiers were dreadfully wounded too. But Dick's determined men managed to hold off the enemy until back-up arrived. Dick was rescued and rushed to hospital in a nearby town called Caserta. He became so ill that it looked as if he would never see Myrle again.

A part-time poet

As a young man, Dick never wrote stories or dreamed of being an author. However, as a hobby in his spare time, he did enjoy writing poetry. He wrote one poem, entitled *Eighty-eight Shell*, about a bomb that exploded and killed two of his guardsmen during the war.

A farm and a family

Dick's life was saved by a new medicine called penicillin. After several months, he recovered enough to be sent to a hospital in Liverpool back in England. Imagine how joyful Dick and Myrle were to see each other again!

When Dick left hospital, the couple went to live at Dick's parents' house in Bitton. There, Dick spent the next two years slowly getting back to health.

A soldier no longer

In October 1945, just after the end of the war, Dick and Myrle had a baby girl, Juliet. Dick moved his family to a tiny old cottage in the Wylye Valley. While Myrle looked after the baby, Dick went back to work on Tytherington Farm. However, Dick still dreamed of having a farm of his own. In the autumn of 1946, he went to college to study farming. A year later, he was a qualified farmer at last.

Baby Juliet's christening. Myrle is holding Juliet and Dick is behind her, surrounded by their parents and grandparents.

A rapidly growing family

Dick's family's **paper mill** had a canteen that needed a regular supply of milk and eggs. So they bought nearby Woodlands Farm and put Dick in charge of it. Dick, Myrle and Juliet moved in in early 1948. Just a couple of months later a second daughter, Liz, was born.

Dick and Myrle filled the farm with pets, including dogs, cats and rabbits. As for farm animals, they bought dairy cows, pigs, goats, chickens, ducks and geese. In August 1953, their son Giles was born.

▲ Susie, one of Dick's favourite pets.

It was very hard work. Myrle had the children and pets to take care of, as well as the farmhouse and the garden. Dick had only a cowman to help him with all the farm animals and the different daily jobs. But the couple loved their busy, outdoor life.

The seeds of a story

The day after Liz was born, Dick discovered a disaster in his chicken run. A crafty fox had dug a tunnel underneath the wire-net fence of his chicken coop. It had stuck its nose far enough in to snap at all the panicking chickens and had killed all but three of the birds. Dick vowed that one day he would write a story where strong creatures are beaten by weak creatures. The idea stayed in his head for nearly 20 years until he wrote *The Fox Busters*.

Putting pen to paper

While Dick was farming, he sometimes did a little writing for fun. He once wrote about how he had seen a badger one morning. He had almost got close enough to touch it! Dick sent the **article** to a magazine called *The Countryman*, but they did not **publish** it.

Another time, Dick wrote some songs with the help of a friend who could play the piano. They wanted to turn them into a **musical**, to be performed in theatres. Sadly, nothing came of the idea.

Dick was still writing poems too. He had better luck with these. He sometimes sent them in to magazines like *Good Housekeeping*, and a few appeared in print. But Dick never thought of making up stories for children.

◀ Dick's favourite pig was called Monty.

Animal characters

Dick and Myrle loved every animal on their farm. They gave them all names to match their personalities. The cows included sensible Buttercup, bad-tempered Kicker and fearful Cissie. The pigs included a monster-sized male called Monty. Dick came to be especially fond of pigs. He realized that, like humans, pigs eat both meat and vegetables, they like to be clean, they are greedy, and they are very clever!

Failing at farming

Dick was excellent with animals, but no good at all at making money. For instance, the cows Dick chose for his dairy herd did not produce enough milk. When Dick wanted to buy piglets, he did not shop around for a good price but bought expensive ones instead. Dick was also quite accident-prone. His machinery and equipment often seemed to go wrong or fall apart, which meant costly repairs.

In 1961 the paper mill closed down. Dick had to move to a different farm called Overscourt, just a few miles away. This farm was even bigger, so it was even harder for Dick to run. By 1967, he had made no money at all. He was forced to sell everything and give up farming.

▲ Dick's family's paper mill was like this one. This man is counting sheets of paper by hand.

The stories start to flow

Dick was 45 years old and had been a farmer for 20 years. Whatever was he to do now? Instead of getting up early to milk the cows, he had nothing to roll out of bed for. Worst of all, what was the family going to do for money? It was a very worrying time.

The first problem was finding somewhere to live. Luckily, a friend owned an empty cottage and said that Dick and the family could stay there for free. Then another friend offered Dick a job for six months, travelling about selling fire-fighting suits. After that, Dick went to work in a shoe factory in Bristol. He did not much like that and after three years he left. Once more, Dick did not know what to do next.

▲ Dick really disliked working in a shoe factory like this one.

Dick tries teaching

A friend suggested that Dick would make a good teacher. Dick liked the idea! So at the age of 49, he became a student again. Dick began a three-year teacher training course at Bristol University. He enjoyed it so much that he stayed on for an extra year to study for a degree.

▲ Farmborough Primary School, where Dick was a teacher.

At last, Dick was happy again. He and Myrle moved into a lovely old house called Diamond's Cottage, in Somerset – just a few miles from where he was born. Then Dick began teaching at nearby Farmborough Primary School. He loved helping children read and write and learn. The only thing Dick did not enjoy was teaching maths, because he was not good with numbers!

School sparks off a story

Farmborough Primary School building was partly modern and partly very old. One of the old classrooms Dick taught in was so leaky that rain came in through the roof! Many years later, he used the classroom for the setting of a story called *The Schoolmouse*.

A story at last!

As a teacher, Dick now had long summer holidays. During his first summer break in 1976, he finally kept the promise he had made to himself 20 years before on his first farm. He wrote a story inspired by his experience of a fox attacking his chickens. Dick sent the tale to a couple of **publishers** who turned it down. But the third publisher liked it! They turned the story into Dick's first book, *The Fox Busters*.

▲ The cover of Dick's first book, *The Fox Busters*.

▲ An illustration from Dick's book *Magnus Powermouse*.

Writing takes over

Dick was delighted. He set about working on more stories straight away. He wrote his first tale about a pig, *Daggie Dogfoot*, then *The Mouse Butcher* and *Magnus Powermouse*. Dick's ideas were coming so thick and fast, he did not have enough spare time from teaching to write them all! Then, sadly, in 1980, Dick's parents both died. With the money they left him, Dick was able to give up teaching and concentrate on his writing. He had a tiny study built upstairs at Diamond's Cottage and became a full-time author.

What Dick says

This is how Dick once described becoming a writer:

'*When first you learn to ride a bike, you fall off quite a lot, and the same goes for learning anything quite new, like writing books for children. I had some false starts and made a lot of booboos, but ... I found, once I'd buckled down to the job, that I had masses of ideas for stories and that I was getting a whole lot of fun writing them.*'

Going from strength to strength

Dick's first four books were all animal tales. Next, he used his wacky imagination to dream up a story about magic, called *The Queen's Nose*. His sixth book, *The Sheep-Pig*, flew off the shelves of bookshops and won a top prize called the Guardian's Children's Fiction Award. Dick suddenly had to get used to being one of the most famous, best-loved children's writers in Britain. Fans everywhere wanted to see him at school visits and appearances at bookshops and libraries.

No stopping the story-teller

Since then, Dick has written many more wonderful stories about animals and the people who love them, such as the *Sophie* stories, *Martin's Mice* and *Dodos Are Forever*. He has also dreamed up other magical tales, such as *The Witch of Blackberry Bottom* and *The Magic Carpet Slippers*. Recently, Dick has told tales for older readers too: *Godhanger* and *The Crowstarver*.

▲ Dick and his dog, Dodo, became TV presenters!

▲ The movie *Babe* was based on Dick's book *The Sheep-Pig*.

On-screen

As a well-known author, Dick appeared in the 1980s on three children's TV programmes – *Rub-a-dub-tub*, *Pob's Programme* and *Tumbledown Farm* – talking about animals. He thought that TV presenting was good fun, but he did not enjoy it as much as writing. In 1995 Dick saw his work on the big screen when *The Sheep-Pig* was turned into a Hollywood movie. This movie, *Babe*, was a huge hit in many different countries and won Dick even more fans. Recently, *The Queen's Nose* and the *Sophie* stories have also been made into successful TV programmes.

What the newspapers say

Here is some praise for Dick from book reviews in newspapers:

'*a fine and funny writer*'
    Nicolette Jones, the *Independent*, 8 October 2001

'*loved ... for dozens of excellent books*'
    Christina Hardyment, the *Independent*, 22 September 2001

'*a joy to read*'
    Julia Eccleshare, the *Guardian*, 10 November 2001

The successful author

Today, Dick is an elderly man who enjoys a quiet life at home. He says that he has slowed down a lot as he has got older and now likes being lazy! However, he still writes nearly every day, because he enjoys it so much.

A typical day in the life of Dick King-Smith

In the morning, Dick settles in his upstairs study. It is so small that if he sits in his chair and stretches his arms out to the sides, he can touch both walls at once! Dick works for a couple of hours, thinking a lot and then scribbling away with a pen on rough paper. In the afternoon, he types up what he has written on an old typewriter. It is a slow process, because Dick uses just one finger! But this gives him the chance to make changes and corrections as he goes along. Later, Dick likes to relax by pottering about in his garden, or sitting in a big comfy chair, thinking up new ideas for stories.

Animal magic

One of the things Dick enjoys most about writing stories is imagining how animals might talk. He is careful never to turn his characters into humans. They always talk and act like the animals they are. Here is how Babe talks to the sheep in *The Sheep-Pig*:

'I want to be a sheep-pig,' he said.
'Ha ha!' bleated a big lamb standing next to Ma. 'Ha ha ha-a-a-a-a!'
'Be quiet!' said Ma sharply, swinging her head to give the lamb a thumping butt in the side. 'That ain't nothing to laugh at.'

This is how Dick once described how he works:

'I write in all the wrong ways. I don't plan a story out as I should, I just get an idea and blast off into the wild blue yonder, hoping that things will turn out OK and that it will eventually have what all successful stories must have ... a Good Beginning, a Good Middle and a Good End. Usually it works, sometimes it doesn't, but it suits me.'

Ideas from real life

Dick's ideas sometimes come from real people and actual experiences. For instance, once at a village fête, Dick was put in charge of the 'Guess-the-weight-of-the-piglet' stall. Wondering what was going to happen to the piglet gave him the idea for *The Sheep-Pig*. For his *Sophie* stories, Dick based the determined, animal-loving Sophie on his wife Myrle, and turned his own Great-aunt Al into Sophie's Great-great aunt Alice!

▲ Dick and his trusty old typewriter!

Dick King-Smith on Dick King-Smith

Here are some of Dick's answers to questions we asked him:

What is your house, Diamond's Cottage, like?
'Very small and very old. We've been told that it was built over 350 years ago. We made it a bit bigger in the 1980s by adding a dining room and a new bathroom, as well as my study. I love sitting in my garden.'

What do you think makes you a good writer for children?
'I have always hated and feared numbers, but loved words! I know what kind of stories children like, because I taught primary school youngsters for seven years.'

Why have you written so many stories about animals?
'Kids love animals – so they like reading stories about animals too. And I know enough about animals to write about them without making silly mistakes!'

▲ An illustration from Dick's book *The Sheep-Pig*.

▲ Dick has seen the world by travelling on cruise ships like this one.

Out of all the books you have written, which is your favourite?
'I have always been especially fond of *The Sheep-Pig*, even long before it became a success.'

Did you have anything to do with the making of the movie Babe?
'Nothing at all. I first saw the film with Myrle when it opened at a cinema in London. Farmer Hogget was exactly how I had pictured him in my head! I later went on a three-month **cruise** that visited Australia, and the director of *Babe* took me to where they had made the movie.'

Dick's writing tips

Here is Dick's advice to anyone who wants to become a writer like him:

1) Read as widely as possible – not so you can copy other people's writing style, but it will help you develop your own.

2) Practise! Try writing your own stories.

3) Show your stories to a grown-up you like and trust, such as your mum, step-dad, or a favourite teacher. Listen to what they say and try to take their advice on board.

4) Keep on trying and don't give up!

Dick today

Sadly, when Dick was nearly 78 years old, Myrle died. They had been married for 57 years. In his book *Chewing the Cud*, Dick wrote, 'Without Myrle, I could never have been what I now am.' However, he has lots of grandchildren and great-grandchildren to keep him busy. Dick has also found new happiness by getting married again, to a long-time friend called Zona.

▲ Dick, Myrle and some of their family at Dick's 75th birthday party in 1997.

Home is where the heart is

Dick once said that 'I love the English countryside and would probably die immediately if forced to live in a town'. Today, he is content and happy at Diamond's Cottage and thinks that going anywhere outside the garden gate is a great adventure.

Whenever Dick is talked into going on holiday, he travels to see the world on big, comfortable **cruise** ships. He has been afraid of flying all his life, so he will never travel by aeroplane! Dick sometimes goes on holiday by train, too.

Fans and plans

Every week Dick receives lots of letters from children all over the world who love his stories. Dick thinks this is the best bit about being a writer. He tries to reply to them all. Dick says that he now tends to spend more time snoozing than working. But he still has plenty of ideas for new stories. He enjoys writing too much to stop.

▲ Children all over the world love Dick's stories. Dick is shown here with a reader on the TV programme *Roundabout* in 1989.

> ### What the readers say
>
> **Here is what some fans think about Dick's books:**
>
> '*...great, cool and wicked!*'
>> (A class of Year 3 and Year 4 pupils from Johnstown Junior School, Wrexham, UK, on *The Hodgeheg*)
>
> '*Sophie and her friends are a delight to the imagination...*'
>> (Lottie, aged 9, from Canterbury, Kent, UK on the *Sophie* stories)
>
> '*A brilliant story!*'
>> (Samuel, aged 8, from Guernsey, on *The Sheep-Pig*)

Timeline

1922 Dick is born

1941 Joins the **army** to fight in **World War II**

1943 Marries Myrle England (with whom he has three children)

1947–1967 Works as a farmer

1975 Begins work as a primary school teacher

1978 *The Fox Busters* is **published**

1982 Gives up teaching to be a full-time writer

1984 *The Sheep-Pig* wins the Guardian's Children's Fiction Award

1992 Dick is voted Children's Author of the Year

1995 *Harriet's Hare* wins the Children's Book Award

   The Sheep-Pig is turned into the movie *Babe*

2000 Myrle dies

2001 Dick marries old friend Zona

Books by Dick King-Smith

Here are some books by Dick you might like to read:

The Fox Busters (Gollancz, 1978)
   Some foxes get a surprise when the chickens they attack decide to fight back!

Magnus Powermouse (Gollancz, 1982)
   Magnus is a baby mouse with a huge appetite, who keeps getting bigger and bigger and bigger…

The Sheep-Pig (Gollancz, 1983)
   The story of a pig called Babe who wanted to be a sheep-dog.

Sophie's Snail (Walker Books, 1988)
   The first of six stories about a little girl called Sophie who wants to be a farmer when she grows up.

Glossary

Air Force soldiers trained to fight in aeroplanes

army soldiers trained to fight on foot and in tanks

article piece of writing published in a newspaper or magazine

boarding school school where pupils stay and live during term-time

critic person whose job is to read a story (or see a film or some other entertainment) and write their opinion of it

cruise a trip on a huge, comfortable ship, to see several different countries

enlist to join one of the armed services, for example the Army or Air Force

government the group of people who officially run a country

hand grenade a small hand-held bomb

hoe break up heavy soil with a special long-handled tool

homesick missing home and family very much

musical type of play which includes songs and dancing

paper mill paper-making factory

platoon organized group of soldiers

publish to produce and sell books. A company that publishes books is called a publisher. A published writer is one whose books are sold in shops.

World War II war that lasted from 1939 to 1945. It began when Germany marched its army into Poland.

Index

animal stories 4, 5, 15, 20, 21, 22, 25, 26

Babe (movie) 4, 23, 27
Bitton 6, 14

Chewing the Cud 11, 28
The Crowstarver 22

Daggie Dogfoot 21
Diamond's Cottage 19, 21, 26, 28
Dodos Are Forever 22

The Fox Busters 4, 15, 20, 30

Godhanger 22

The Hodgeheg 4

ideas for stories 4, 21, 25

King-Smith, Dick
  awards 4, 22
  childhood 6–9
  factfile 5
  family 6, 7
  farming 4, 10, 11, 14, 15, 16, 17
  interview questions 26–7
  marriage and children 12–13, 14, 15, 28
  movies 23, 29
  pet animals 5, 6, 8, 15, 22
  poetry 13, 16
  schooldays 8
  song-writing 16
  teaching career 19, 21
  timeline 30
  TV presenter 22, 23
  wartime service 12, 13

writing career 4, 15, 16, 20–2, 23, 26–7, 29
  writing method 24, 25
King-Smith, Giles (son) 15
King-Smith, Juliet (daughter) 14
King-Smith, Liz (daughter) 15
King-Smith, Myrle (wife) 9, 11, 12–13, 28
Kipling, Rudyard 5

The Magic Carpet Slippers 22
magical stories 22
Magnus Powermouse 21, 30
Martin's Mice 22
The Mouse Butcher 21

Overscourt 17

The Queen's Nose 22, 23

readers' comments 29
reviewers 23

The Schoolmouse 19
The Sheep-Pig 4, 22, 23, 24, 25, 26, 27, 30
Sophie stories 4, 22, 23, 25, 30

TV presenting 23
Tytherington Farm 10, 12, 14

The Witch of Blackberry Bottom 22
Woodlands Farm 15
World War II 10, 12, 13
writing tips 27

Titles in the *All About Authors* series are:

All about...
Malorie Blackman

Shaun McCarthy

Hardback   0 431 17982 4

All about...
Rob Childs

Shaun McCarthy

Hardback   0 431 17986 7

All about...
Roald Dahl

Vic Parker

Hardback   0 431 17981 6

All about...
Anne Fine

Vic Parker

Hardback   0 431 17987 5

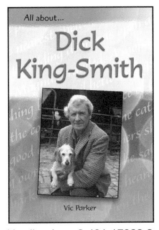

All about...
Dick King-Smith

Vic Parker

Hardback   0 431 17988 3

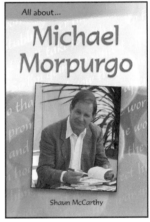

All about...
Michael Morpurgo

Shaun McCarthy

Hardback   0 431 17985 9

All about...
J.K. Rowling

Shaun McCarthy

Hardback   0 431 17980 8

All about...
Jacqueline Wilson

Vic Parker

Hardback   0 431 17983 2

Find out about the other titles in this series on our website www.heinemann.co.uk/library